WHISPERS OF A SNOWFALL

CELEBRATING THE PENSIVE BEAUTY OF WINTERS...

RASHIKA RANJINI

Made with ♥ on the Notion Press Platform
www.notionpress.com

Mr. P, I was living life resembling the last words of some random dying character in Assassins Creed II - "I feel no fear, assassin. Only regret."

You showed me what life could be about.

This book is dedicated to you, and the spring you bring to my winters.

Contents

Acknowledgements — *vii*

1. Sky Carpet — 1
2. The Strange Seller At Snowslope — 2
3. Signorina M. Winter — 5
4. Chants Of Snowflakes — 6
5. Apricity, How Do I Love Thee? — 8
6. An Icicle Cycle — 9
7. Prophecy Of A Winter Stone — 10
8. An Epic Couplet — 11
9. Frost Flowers — 12
10. Winter Birds — 13
11. Snow-crostic — 14
12. An Ode To Christmas — 15
13. A Candy Cane Carol — 16
14. Gingerbread Canopy — 17
15. Rudolph Ruminates — 18
16. Whilst We're Apart — 19
17. The Formidable Snowstorm — 20
18. A Clement Farewell — 21
19. Ringing Spring In — 22

Acknowledgements

Thanking these souls that the angels decided I deserve in my life:

* My dear dad, who may no longer be with me in body, but will always be with me in spirit, inspiring me in ways more than words can ever express;

* My darling mom, who's always been my rock, my pillar, and my lifeboat through many a winterstorm;

* My sweet daughter, whose laughter fills my heart so much.

Your love, guidance, and support have meant a hell lot to me, and without these, this book would have been completed in half the time it originally took (really, try writing a paragrah, leave alone a book, with my mom and daughter in the same room), but would have turned out be like a dry and dreary sunless pine forest.

1. Sky Carpet

Once a wordless witness
to multitude of conquests,
today the sky is but a canvas
of a million white stars -

Each snowy speck bearing
haunting testimony to life's
never-ceasing profusion of changes...

Every luminous flake ferrying
the burdens of the evening
to the banks of the morning...

Each holding the other's hands,
framing an absolute ghostly laminate,
covering the earth's blemishes...

Watching with wise solemnity, as
my feet tread on, seeking
cognizant answers to tomorrow.

2. The Strange Seller At Snowslope

One day at a Winter shop,
I met a man selling some sadness,
For money he wanted to swap,
But I really wanted some madness.

"Got any madness?" asked I.
"For that's how I'll spend my money."
"No madness here!" said the guy.
He seemed to find it quite funny.

"We've got some lovely joy capsules,"
He offered, "I'll give you a very fine price."
"I'd rather have some lunacy pills," I replied..
The man blinked rapidly thrice.

The man seemed exceptionally brainy,
And his manner, that of one strangely amused.
He wasn't what I would call zany, but great
Contempt to my questions he noticeably oozed.

Like others, he thought I was odd,
Some say I'm quite eccentric.
Still he gave me a courteous nod,
As if he thought I was plenty prosaic.

So in search of my goal I departed,
But before the Winter shop could I leave,
The man came running full-hearted,
"I can help you I believe."

"Madness you shall find, and
Insanity, you can get.
You must now open your mind,
And get down to Snowslope Market."

So to Snowslope Market I decided to go,
In search of the madness I craved.
The winds did eerily blow,
But I felt that the day could be saved.

There were stalls selling
Rings of joy in many a shade
There were even stalls selling
Wings of hope claimed to never fade

I was greeted by a peculiar lady,
She seemed to be rather tall and I couldn't
Help thinking that the shop was a tad shady.
I wondered if she was at all cool.

Before I could open my mouth,
She shouted, "For you, I have some madness!"
I headed towards her, to the south,

Past some joy and hope.

"But how did you know?" I asked,
"Do you want this or not?" she did say.
Silently, the madness she passed.
Then vanished before I could pay.

As I walked away I hard a crackle
Or was it, perhaps, a hushed cackle?

3. Signorina M. Winter

Dressed in the divine demeanour of serenity,
Her face clothed in the pallor of burden
From the the cognizance - of
Grievous pasts and callous sins - of
Heinous crimes and gruesome wins - of
Wishful hopes and blurry resolutions - all
Summing up the year that she has witnessed.

She sways and snorts, as she grapples
With what has come to be reality,
Masking her anguish inside with,
The efficient cloak of indifference.

Onward she strolls, hiding
Her sorrows within, and flaunting
Her insouciance without.

A smirk dances on her lips,
As she recalls the first name on her
Nametag - Merciless.

4. Chants of Snowflakes

Fallen -
Is what the unknowledgeable
Would say - when
They see us descend
From the skies and dance
Merrily on smiling grounds...

Fragile -
Is what the unimaginative
Would say - as they our
Resplendent White attire and
Iridescent silver crowns...

Forgotten -
Is what the unenlightened
Would say - as their minds bundle away
Our magnificence into three
Months of their calendars...

Little do they know of our
Magic - that remains invisible to
Those seeking to survive mere
Rat races...

We may seem ephemeral, but

We are spectators to all
That is beholden in this
Universe - silent reminders of
Hope and perseverance.

5. Apricity, how do I love Thee?

How do I love thee? Let me count the ways.
The wind stopped to listen from the moor;
Every leaf of foliage laid on the trees vanish,
Their purpose carved on them for a garden of gold;
Since I came to the forsaken land upon Vermont,
And combed the daylight for hidden hoary acorns,
You shone on me in a dream of an idle night,
Lording my ideals and aims then on.
You came like the dazzling light for a moment,
And later as the shadow of a graceful enchanter.
You told me to not dwell on the pomace of the past,
But to conquer the looming mountains.
How do I love thee? - In the only way I know of,
With weathered words of my regal worship.

6. An Icicle Cycle

She looks at the sheen of her robe, with
A narrow stare, reticent to the call.
The moon with her flame against the sky,
She stood on her fence against the wall.

She bade a warm smile at the full night,
Silent and white with the heavy snow,
Black secrets shrouded outta sight,
Away she grappled with her woe!

Amidst the smile of a friend's new beam,
She knew it was time to alight her throne.
Day and evening made but a troubled dream,
She melted, with the fire of her smile to own.

7. Prophecy of a Winter Stone

Whose stone is that? I think I know.
Its owner is quite happy though.
Full of joy like a vivid rainbow,
I watch her laugh as I wave her a hello.

She gives her stone a shake,
And laughs until her frizzled brows ache.
The only other sound's the break,
Of distant waves and birds awake.

She rises from her gentle bed.
Young shines the day thru' victories red.
She knows that the stone must a purpose have,
As does every being held by Earth's grav.

The stone is bouncy, pensive and shiny,
As she claws it around in search of a key.
When none she finds, with a dark look of agony,
She embraces a premonition of adversity.

8. An Epic Couplet

Sneaking into the new year

As the air rings a note of cheer,

Winter muses to her pine friend

That music never escorts her end,

And that no angel sings of her to a bee.

"Ne'er doth twilight stay to visit me,

And neither doth the night spark

Her eyes when I enter," she wailed from her mark.

The pine, brushing off her snowy powder

Smiled as her sad indignation got louder.

Dust and darkness sang upon her cheek,

Bathed in her beauty, painted sharp and sleek.

"I await you like the sea awaits the flood,

As the dawn awaits a ship long hulled.

You come to me as a radiant wave - when my seclusion

Glimmers and roars through its haunted cave.

You are all I envision all through summer and fall

Through the grand dances of the moon and all."

As he concludes, she glances up at him, the smiling pine.

Her white song swirls, "Pray thanks to those words of thine."

9. Frost Flowers

"Can your grim beauty have a contender?"
I question the frost flowers, as they shake the smoke off.
I see the snowflakes astride the lamp of the fender,
Whilst I wait for their cold and unpitying scoff.
"We may not gleam with the lilies in their white beard,
Nor will we march on to their native abode,
But we carry beauty in our remorse," they me cheered,
As I blinked, lost like a caique at a winding road.
Their chuckles gracefully ascended the ladder of evening air.
"We are fierce like the flaming Mercury, and at times may be
Crisp, like the souls of a midnight street," they said in compare.
"But we are not unwarm to festive joy." Their words console me.
As I see them, sitting kingly upon their cold height,
I wonder how some lives can smile and some naught be;
Lodged with the knowing, and a pale but longing despair of delight,
I tell myself that frost flowers can devour my eyes any day, than a lily

10. Winter Birds

Glad rime nips at the robins of December,
Hovering over the towering solemn woods.
"Winter lass, who'd thee love the most?"
They ask her in unison, for which she remarks,
"Cadinal, I love the kindness from thy bright eyes,
Junco, my dreams shall form thy memory as a star.
Woodpecker, thou behold thy golden throne upright,
And ye Goldfinch, thy guise resembles the Lar.
Nuthatch, beside thy wings, does the moon totter,
And Chickadee, thou smile like a fair roseate parterre.
Sparrows and Jays, I drown in thy shy chirp and cries.
Oh, but who amongst ye should reign over my skies?"
"Methinks thou shan't need a ruler," I quip,
Eager to state my stance and have my voice heard.
"Thou art the ruler, and thou art the ruled.
Why would thou let birds wear thy crown?"
She beams and bids us all goodbye,
While the birds and I linger on.

11. Snow-crostic

Snowdrifts wade through, with the

Nocturnal whistles crying shrill.

Ominous clouds obscured from

Wistful beams of the Sun sorcerer.

Fiery mists overcast the noon, whilst

Alpine snowdrifts trudge onward.

Little flurries form a sleet, and the

Leaden clouds withdraw their veil.

12. An Ode to Christmas

My joyful Christmas, you embolden me to write.
Uplifting with the light of human skies,
You glide silently into our depths by night,
Shining the silvery spirit of thine eyes.
Instilling in us the flair for giving,
Incandescently you wash the world aglow.
Showing us to gather the good for a joyous living,
Meeting the moon above from our demesne below.

13. A Candy Cane Carol

"I am a cane with a difference," I brag,
Bathing in the oven's glow at the fair array.
I count my friends sailing into the Christmas bag,
Each of them, to add blessing to a child's day.
We sing in joy, seeing a bow in the flower below,
Dancing in the flames from the very comfortable fire.
We mutter, shaking the world from its idle sorrow,
Preening in our dressing and regal delicious attire.
Afore, the kitchen is in full sparkle and glory.
We sit down in glorious tire, like many a warrior.
Fashioned with mini trees, happily green as the prairie,
We await the eve, as eagerly as the rest of the quartier.

14. Gingerbread Canopy

Not long now,
Before these brown sheets
Are ready to make delectable
Houses and towns...

I take in the whiffs of
these toothsome treats -
Savoring these moments
of longing and yearning
before these turn into
Abodes that get devoured...

Sweet here and hot there,
I adorn these with
Flattering outfits of icing
And sprinkle them with
Silver sugar...

Not long now,
Before these are ready
For Crunchy battles.

15. Rudolph Ruminates

Invading the white skies in the night,

I get my troop to pull the sleigh.

An angel flies by, with an eye for the right,

She sails with the clouds upon her way.

My nose blushed with the golden light of divinity,

My cries piercing the glowing young air,

The flaming town begone behind me,

I gallop to the whip of that majestic chair.

Half behind my smiles, I bore a lot of gifts and glee,

As the next town gleams white in the haze.

My thoughts go frolicking forth in this liberty,

And I sight the next chimney through the concrete maze.

16. Whilst We're Apart

"Remember my bright words whilst we're apart."

She rests her words on the startled ledge,

As she waits for the sierras to answer.

As they wake up from their white slumber,

She seeks their mammoth forms with a double wave.

In their broad shoulders, carrying a valley of grief,

They eagerly await the blue touch of her smile.

"I'll be back before you know it," says her cheering tone.

"But good days are 'round the corner!"

She reminds them from atop her glittering crest.

As she takes off, feeding a song to the tarnished night,

They await - her return, and the banquet of her presence.

17. The Formidable Snowstorm

The prayers are doused by the deafening snowstorm
"What witless memo could this be bringing forth?"
Wonders my inept mind in its golden mesh of youth.
I turn my gaze away to look yonder at the mount of tears.
Shaken and tremoring with fear, the mount looks on.
As I look back at the snowstorm and its now happy air,
It dawns on me that the snowstorm is feared,
not by the world's joy or the summer sky,
But by the sorrow shared by the souls near and afar.
As the snowstorm washes away its ocean of ashes,
The mount stands forlorn, robbed of its cloak of tears,
And the now happy land smiles with hopes renewed.

18. A Clement Farewell

I wish to bid a sonorous adieu,

Persevering like a bridge of sheen and magic.

But drawn by the light of the glorious sunset,

I forget my words, both joyful and tragic.

I glimmer and roar through the open night,

Hoping to find the lines lost from mind and sight.

The forest, as ever deaf to the lake of deep emotion,

Witnesses, crossing its arms in a deft motion.

I decide to try one last time, clear and loud,

As I call for my words through the conifer crowd.

"You leave your mark in the season's spirit,

And that's why your presence - we revere it!"

As a booming voice disrupts the poem of the air,

I look up at the ray, grateful for its comforting glare.

Alighting the stairway to Heaven, I look cheerfully back,

And whisper, "Don't take your sorrows back from wrack."

19. Ringing Spring In

Spring is my name, and I am off to work
I run with a resonating melody, and a
Burning shade of luminosity, as I
Swim through the currents of splendour.
I catch a glimpse of the departing Winter,
Her suit turning purple from a Sun splinter.
Remnants of her tail swimming hither,
Like those of a mellow dragon in the wind thither.